POWERING STARTUPS FROM 1 TO 10^6X BY GROWTH HACKING

Exponential Growth Driver for Startups & Digital Marketers

Amar Jyoti

CONTENTS

PREFACE

Being in a lockdown due to the global pandemic, has its own share of positives out of all the negativity around, you do get a lot of time to introspect about the current state you are in and retrospect regarding your life's journey. Personally for me it gave wings to a long standing whim of penning down something which can add some value to the lives of many.

Being in the Startup ecosystem for some time, I realized that though we have a lot of course materials, tutorials and theoretical books available in the sphere of startups and digital marketing, there are hardly any, which talks about practical hands-on experiences. One has to do a lot of experiments, A/B testing, Optimization etc. to arrive at the best practices across marketing channels especially when you are just starting up. This made me pen down a few of those best practices from my experiences in the form of a handbook intended for the greater good of the Startup Enthusiasts and Growth Marketer folks.

Once you decide and have the will to do something, the greatest obstacle is in the mind. Once you get over this hurdle you have to figure out ways to give shape to your plans. For me, I found a great ally in Amazon which not only provides you the platform to sell your book, but also helps you with all the tools to format your book, create a cover image for your book etc. Being my first handbook, I didn't want to go overboard with the design and investments aspect, so Amazon was a perfect platform for me to experiment with the Author in me.

Being an Electrical Engineer and MBA graduate, I started my career with some of India's top Brands - Tata Technologies & ICICI Bank. But my inclination towards Startup hustle dragged me out of the steady corporate world. Thereby I joined Fastfox, a home rental startup as a Core Founding member and donned the hat of 'Head of Growth'. I was lucky to be mentored by a couple of top names in the Startup ecosystem, Mr Pallav Pandey, a Serial entrepreneur and ex Knowlarity Founder and Mr Anshul Gupta, an Internet entrepreneur.

On the foundation of a super charged team and backed by some of the top Venture Capitalists, we went on to build a Tech-Enabled high class product offering and eventually got acquired at a Valuation of 1 Billion by Elara Technologies.

Post Fastfox, I did a Political Consultancy stint working in close tandem with an Union Minister of India for the General Elections 2019. Post that, I headed the Growth Vertical in one of India's top mid-sized startups Housing.com. Currently, I am heading the Growth vertical at Square Yards, India's largest real estate platform and leading them in their Growth Path. This book is based on my practical hands-on experiences working across different industries and organizations over all these years.

INTRODUCTION

Thank you for having decided to give this handbook a read which happens to be my first. Well to set expectations at the outset, this book does not talk much about theoretical aspects of Marketing rather it is a short handbook of practical techniques for digital marketers and founders who want to accelerate their personal growth or growth of their startup's.

The handbook speaks about some of the effective Marketing techniques, growth hacks and best practices that I have uncovered during my hands on experience and association with early stage startups over the years. This book is mostly about practical applications and speaks about some of the best practices used over Marketing platforms like Google, Linkedin, Facebook, Whatsapp & SMS.

For accomplishing any small or big task, one thing I have realised over the years - 'It's all in the mind'. It's a 3 step decision making process with mind as the Decision maker.

Each one of us encounter a myriad of crazy thoughts and ideas which we want to accomplish. These thoughts can be big or small, of any kind & related to any sphere. This essentially forms the Input which is further processed.

Step 1: Does it overlap with your current interests or passions. 90% thoughts are killed at this stage.

Step 2: Does it overlap with your strengths & weaknesses ? In short, do you genuinely believe you can crack it.

Step 3: Final step where one does the effort/cost vs benefit analysis.

Once it's through all the 3 screening steps, nothing should stop an individual in conquering it, provided one has the appetite for success, is aware of the best practices in place and executes them well.

Best practices can be learnt over time from Books, You Tube Videos, Blogs, LinkedIn and many other places but the essence lies wholly in execution. One needs to apply the techniques themselves to be confident about them. All the growth hacking ideas that I am going to talk about in this book are results of hands down experience. You might be already aware about some of them but if you can pick 4-5 new things from the entire book and implement it well, I would be highly delighted as my purpose of penning down the book will be solved.

CHAPTER 1: GROWTH HACKING

The term 'Growth Hacking' is a relatively new addition to the corporate dictionary. Even the keyword planner will apprise you of the fact that the search volume of this particular keyword is quite moderate. You will find chief marketing officers (CMO), digital marketers and marketing specialists in organizations but rarely you will find organizations who have a dedicated growth team or a chief growth officer (CGO).

So what exactly is 'Growth Hacking' and do organizations need such a team ?

There are multiple ways to accomplish any task, but growth hacking will enable you to approach and find a solution to the problem by taking the shortest possible route.

Startups live by day and they have a limited runway in terms of budget to spare with. It really becomes imperative for them to explore growth hacks to sustain and achieve exponential growth in a frugal manner. Once the organization grows big, often the focal point shifts towards managing and running current businesses. This makes it really critical even for the larger organizations to have a growth team in place for having an eye on the future innovations and making sure they do not turn obsolete by keeping pace with time.

What does it require to be a 'Growth Hacker' ?

Anyone and everyone can be a growth hacker. For being a growth hacker you need to be able to think out of the box and do not get curtailed by drawn boundaries and limits. You are expected to be the problem solver and come up with innovative practical solutions to business problems.

Apart from attitude you need to develop skill sets and have a good amount of working knowledge across multiple functions like product, marketing and operations. You are not expected to be experts in these domains but you need to be thorough about the concepts and have a sound technical knowledge. You should have a keen appetite to learn with a constant need to upgrade and upskill yourselves.

Being the agent of change you are expected to drive innovations in the traditional ways the business operates by working with cross functional teams. You need to inculcate the virtues of patience and persistence, as at times you might have to face resistance while bringing in a change. This makes it imperative for you to gain the trust of all the stakeholders for any specific task and take them into confidence by briefing them about the benefits of the pilot that you are undertaking. Few people might still feel insecure and threatened, ignore them and march ahead as you have a bigger battle to win.

Trust me growth hacking is one the most interesting career profiles you can land up with. You are exposed to new challenges and problem sets at regular intervals, which makes sure your work is not one dimensional and mundane.

CHAPTER 2: REACTIVE ORGANISATIONAL CULTURE

In this chapter I would like to highlight a key organizational virtue that forms the foundation for building up a successful organization from scratch.

The cut-throat competitive market that we are in, with a new startup springing up virtually every single day, it has become really imperative for businesses to be on their toes. Either you live up to the pressure, innovate and stay competitive or you perish. This is not only restricted to businesses alone but also valid for employees looking to fast track their growth curve. Make sure when you are starting up you have the right mix of such dynamic go-getter set of employees with a couple of experienced leaders to mentor and guide them.

Why do you need to react?

From my own experiences, I have realized one thing - 'you have to respond, you got to react'. Innovation is the mantra of the day. You may be doing pretty well in your space, but you simply cannot stay put and wait for things to take its own course. Bigger organizations have a bureaucratic structure where approvals and selling your ideas through does take its own toll on the time factor. This is the only critical edge which the startups have over the bigger organization as in a startup every single hour counts. Startups live by days, they are nimble-footed and do not enjoy the luxury of fancy funded budgets to have an extended runway. If you are not doing it, then there is someone else lurking somewhere with the hunger and appetite to take the industry leader down. And trust me there are countless examples in the past where the David's of the industries have taken down the Goliath's.

Signals from Daily life

There are innumerable cues from our day to day life which acts as a prompt. Customer feedback is the most critical signal that should ideally trigger a response in terms of thought process. I've seen many founders directing customer feedback into their mailboxes and diligently going through each one of them. Many of them actually go through customer comments and user reviews to listen to the voice of the customers. Unless and until you identify the issues and understand the pain points of the customers, you are surely going to bleed business and waste your efforts making something which the customers may not be even in need of. Apart from the inbound cues, one can surely make an outward reach to access the degree of value their product is adding in the end user's life.

Reacting to Signals

The effectiveness of an organization in reacting to the signals is what defines its destiny. There are organizations, in which employees typically take days to even respond to emails or official Whatsapp conversations. An Organization is as good as its employees, this kind of slow responsive attitude can quite easily disseminate in the entire organization leading it to drag along at a snail pace. Therefore I believe responsiveness is something which needs to be one of the core cultural values of an organization. If every employee possesses the DNA which says 'moment is now and there is no tomorrow', then there is nothing which can stop the organization or the employee from fast tracking their growth path.

In today's world, only one question really matters 'What value is your product adding in the customer's life' ? Everything else other than this is simply garbage. To avoid wasted efforts in the wrong direction, many organizations carry on experiments involving MVP (minimum viable product) with limited features, listen to what the customers have to say and respond accordingly. Working in small batches in the product life cycle and choosing agile development process instead of waterfall are a couple of things that organizations turn to in order to keep pace with the evolving customer needs. Once you are past a certain stage, you can have a dedicated innovation team in your startup to ensure that the wheel of innovation keeps on turning. The problem when organizations scale up is many times they become so engrossed in what they have already built that they forget about the rapidly evolving customer needs.

Suggestions for Founders

Responsiveness needs to flow from top to bottom in the organizations. It should be the responsibility of the leaders to set examples for others to follow. It needs to be imbibed as one of the core DNA's of the organization and the HR team should ensure taking it into account while getting a new employee on board (it is really tough to change a lazy laggard into a man of action). Discussions and long meetings are important to chalk out the plans but the onus should equally be on execution. The leader's job does not end by setting up a 30 ft plan, they need to take stock of the execution process with the same degree of enthusiasm as while chalking out the initial plans. How fast you respond to signals, theoretical discussions and execute plans effectively on the ground is what scripts the success stories of startups.

CHAPTER 3: AARRR FRAMEWORK

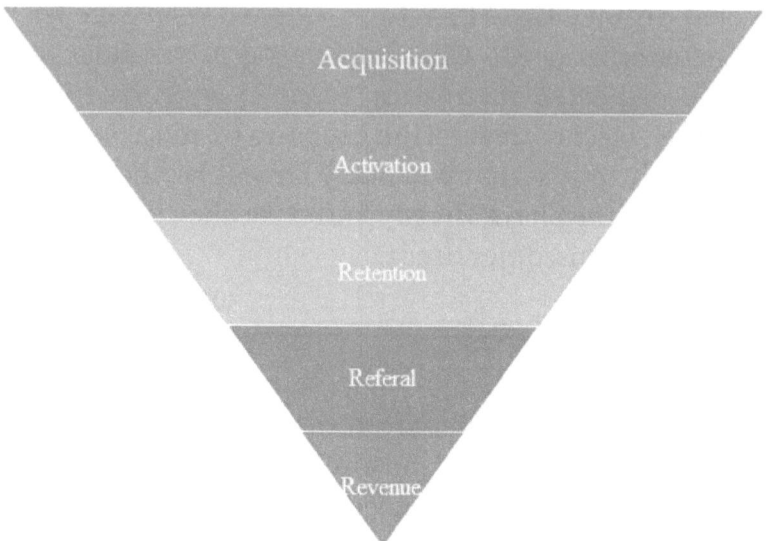

Before I proceed ahead with Marketing tips across platforms, I want to draw your light towards a very essential framework which forms the base for all your marketing efforts. The AARRR funnel framework whose components are

- *Acquisition*

    These are the set of users whom you have acquired through paid campaigns or organic means. It is critical to track all your acquisitions based on source and medium in order to keep the acquisitions cost in check. Track all the channels your acquisitions are coming from (attribution), optimize them and double down on the channels which are working out for you.

- *Activation*

    These are the set of users who have successfully completed

the registration stage (OTP submission, User details form filling etc). Efforts should be made to minimize the drop from Acquisition to Activation stage. If there is a significant drop here, then the possible reasons need to be ascertained and corrective measures needs to be taken.

- *Retention*

   These are the set of users who are actively engaged with your product over a period of time. This is the most important number or metric that any startup founder or marketer should actively track as I believe it is easy to get an user to your Product for the first time, but it is 10 times tougher to retain him. Many founders make the mistake to be elated for the shorter term by tracking the acquisition numbers and ignoring the fact that it's a leaky bucket and their retention numbers are actually dwindling. This number can be tracked by Weekly Cohorts and Metric like Monthly Active Users (MAU).

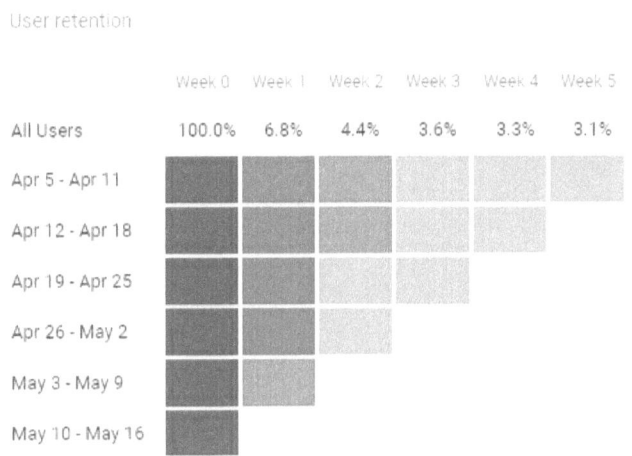

- *Referral*

   These are your valuable users with high customer satisfaction index from among the set of engaged users. They are the source of growing your customer acquisitions organically by Inviting their friends and acquaintances. This is particularly important to keep your Cost per Acquisition (CPA) metric in check.

- *Revenue*

The bottom of the funnel consists of your cream user set who are willing to pay you for your product or services. Every effort should be taken to ensure customer satisfaction for this set of users is at the zenith.

CHAPTER 4: BUILDING RELEVANT DATABASE

Before I jump to Marketing platforms specific discussions, I would like to spend some time by delving into this particular topic which should form the foundation for all your Marketing efforts.

Before spending any Marketing dollars, one needs to specifically identify the target segment for their business. They are essentially the potential customers for your product. Once this is identified then the focus should be on building relevant database comprising this segment. Well there are a lot of ways in which this can be built over time, some of which I would like to broadly give some idea about.

- Reaching out to database companies and vendors. Though the veracity and efficacy of the data from this channel needs to be monitored.

- Some businesses like real estate operate in Whatsapp Groups. If real estate agents are your target segment, try to get into these Groups. Once you are part of the Group, here are the steps that you can follow to compile your data set.

  Step 1: Take the cursor just near to the Group title name, so that all the participants' numbers are visible in a rectangular white box.

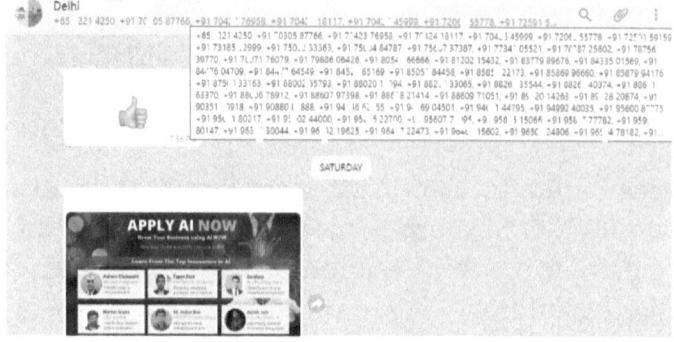

Step 2: Once the rectangular white box starts appearing, click the right mouse button and further click on 'Inspect'. The participants numbers will now start appearing in the new window frame that opens up.

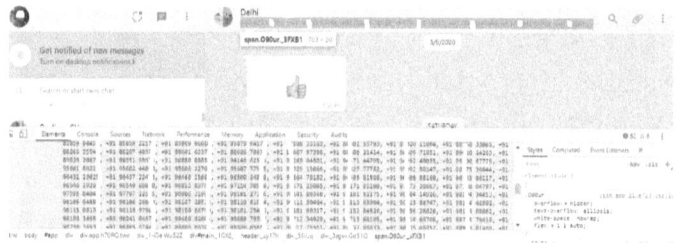

Step 3: Copy the numbers and Paste as Transpose on any Excel Sheet to complete the task.

- You can take premium subscription packages of job portals (with recruiter log in) with unlimited download capability. For example, if your business wants to target HR officials then one can get the requisite data from these portals.

- Search in Google for directories or relevant websites which might contain the info. Figure out automated ways to get the info. Ways of executing the automation script is beyond the scope of this handbook, but just dropping a hint - it can be done by Python language or VBA Script.

- Last but not the least, standard methodology can be applied on Facebook and Google Ads by using the audience building feature through demographics, interests or behavior. Identifying the target segment by employer attribute in Facebook Ads is one of the potent ways to identify relevant audiences as these Ads will only be targeted to people who have updated the concerned employer name in their Profile.

Once you build an audience based on any of the above cited features and run Ads targeting them, it is really imperative to keep on checking and optimizing the attributes of the targeted audiences till you arrive at the perfect combination. One way to check the accuracy is by actually visiting the profiles of the people who are taking any action on your Ad. Actions on your Ads can include post reactions, page likes, post comments etc.

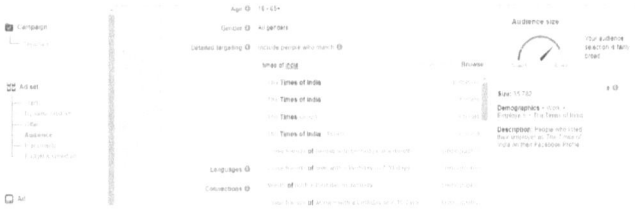

CHAPTER 5: INDEPTH COMPETITOR ANALYSIS & KEYWORD RESEARCH

I t's imperative that you carry out intense research of keywords of your industry and do a comprehensive competitor analysis before jumping on to any means of organic or paid Marketing. Keywords research using tools like Google keyword planner forms the basis of Marketing so I need not delve much in detail about it. But yes, in this chapter I am going to tell you an effective way in which we can make the most out of competitor analysis.

When I say comprehensive competitor analysis, there are 3 aspects of it.

- *Keywords Research*

  Step 1: Identify who your competitors actually are. It can be a long list but you need to pick only 4-5 of them only. The criteria for selection is important. 3-4 of them have to be the top players in your industry for benchmarking whom you want to topple on the long run and 1-2 have to be your nearest competitors whom you would want to overtake in the shorter course.

  Step 2: Once the competitor selection is done, use any of the SEO tools like SEMrush, Ahref etc to identify the keywords which are drawing organic traffic for you and your competitors. Paste them down on separate sheets on a Google spreadsheet. Play with certain words appearing in common on some of these competitor sites. Use the filter option on Google sheet and try to figure out any specific pattern or strategy that appears common and generates sizable traffic for the competitor sites.

Step 3: Once you figure this out try to identify how your competitors are being able to tap into these keywords. Visit those specific competitor pages and try to identify what are the specific elements they are using to tap these keywords. Replicate or better them and you will see the results.

Citing an example which will give you more clarity. "X Type of service near me" or "Y Type of product near me" can be very powerful keyword types in the modern digital era. Suppose one notices a series of "Near Me" pattern type Keywords which is drawing a lot of traffic for your competitors but not for you. Visit your competitor site and identify the elements they are using to tap these set of keywords. It can be by means of page content, meta description or they can be using specific near me type pages to tap into these series of keywords. Once you identify the best practises try to replicate or better them on your site.

- *Backlinks Research*

Step 1: Identify your competitors in the similar lines as cited in the previous section.

Step 2: Use any of the SEO tools like SEMrush, Ahref etc to identify the domains from which you and your competitors are generating a sizable number of backlinks.. Paste them down on separate sheets on a Google Spreadsheet. The domains from which most of your competitors are drawing a good number of backlinks and you are not being able to, are the set of low hanging fruits that you need to tap into immediately.

Step 3: Once you identify these sets of domains, the final step will be to sort them in terms of their domain authority and relevance to your industry. Once this is done the rest is execution of generating backlinks from these domains.

- *Blog Research*

Step 1: Identify your competitors.

Step 2: Use any of the SEO tools like SEMrush, Ahref etc to identify the Blog Articles which are drawing sizable organic traffic for you and your competitors. Paste them down on separate sheets on a Google spreadsheet.

Step 3: Identify the blog topics which are drawing heavy traffic for your competitors. Along with it also jot down the search volumes of the keywords they are able to tap into via these articles.

Step 4: Pick the top 100 blog topics identified in Step 3 and pen down articles in house or you can also outsource the same, targeting the respective keywords as per Step 3.

Step 5: Monitor the progress in terms of traffic and rankings of the blog articles.

CHAPTER 6: CREATING APPEALING CONTENT

C ontent does form one of the most important pillars of Marketing. To stand out from the crowd and to convey your message among your target segment effectively, one needs to follow some of the best practices which I would like to highlight in this chapter.

I would like to classify content into two types

- *Blogging*

    Blogging can be a very powerful tool to draw relevant organic traffic to your site as well as build your brand if used in the right way. Do not create any random content but content which might be genuinely helpful for people of your industry. Content in the form of answers to some of the popular questions, informative articles and infographics are some of the popular content forms which Google loves. I am listing down a few guidelines for generating SEO targeted content which you should keep into account.

    • **Original article**: No plagiarism. Googly loves fresh content and heavily penalizes copy paste stuff.

    • **Well Researched Article**: Research well before jotting down the article. Google the topic and keywords for all available articles over net. Compile your article by taking ideas from all possible sources over the internet.

    • **Avoid Thin Content:** Thin content needs to be avoided. Article needs to be in depth, ideally 1000+ words.

    • **Keywords Density:** Do not overstuff the article with keywords. Make sure the targeted keyword is only 1-2% in Volume, i.e 1 keyword per 100 words. So if it is a 300 word article it should have 3 keywords.

● **Use of Semantics:** Apart from the targeted keywords, similar meaning words or semantics of the keywords can be used at multiple places instead of the main keyword.

● **Heading/Article Title Optimization:** The keyword needs to be towards the starting positions of the article title. It should ideally not be more than 60 characters or 8-12 words.

● **First Paragraph:** Make sure the first paragraph of your article contains the keyword.

● **Interlinking:** Article can contain 2 outbound Links and 2 inbound links to pass on some of the link juice to other articles and vice versa.

● **Anchor Text:** Use relevant anchor texts for linking the articles. It should ideally be the keywords that we are trying to rank the article for.

● **Meta Description:** This should ideally be not more than 180 words and should contain the keywords.

● **URL:** URL needs to contain the keyword.

● **Images & Videos:** Use relevant images and videos wherever possible.

● **Alt Text in Images**: Usage of Alt Texts in all the images used in articles.

● **Social Media Sharing:** Share the article in all possible social media channels.

● **Link Building:** Try to build as many links as possible linked to the article.

- *Paid Ads Content*

Paid Ads content unlike the blogging content needs to be crisp and to the point to catch the attention of the potential customer in the first impression. People generally do not have much attention span to spare for any Marketing Ad. So it is the onus of the marketer to create such a piece of content which can get the customer hooked.

This type of Content can have 3 attributes to it.

- **Hook**: The first line of the content to essentially catch the attention of the customer.

- **Body:** Body of the content to convey the USP or brand value proposition of your product.

- **CTA**: The specific action that you want the user to take after going through your content. It can be to purchase the product, visit your website, fill a lead form or anything.

CHAPTER 7: FACEBOOK GROUPS & PAGES STRATEGY

Going by personal experience, Facebook Groups and Pages can be really effective mediums to drive organic traffic to your website. There are already a ton of Pages and Groups on Facebook out there, so now the question arises how to stand out. This involves taking care of a few basic steps and trying out a few hacks as charted out.

- Do a comprehensive keyword research to identify the most popular keywords in your industry. If people are searching extensively for such keywords on Google, there is a high likelihood of people searching for them on Facebook as well. Pick your Group or Page name from amongst these high volume search keywords.

- Facebook Pages are more likely to spread faster than Groups. Do not limit yourself to just creating a single Page. You can create multiple of them with the most popular keywords as Page names. But when it comes to Group, I will suggest to create only one by choosing your strongest keyword as the Group name. Make the Group & all the created Pages public instead of private. You should aim to put all your focus on growing this Group exponentially in terms of membership. The Pages will slowly and steadily pick pace and grow organically in terms of likes.

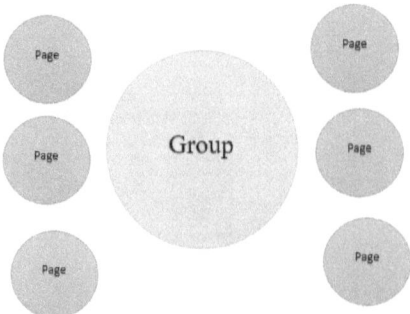

- Complete all other basic steps like About the Page, Tags, Location, Cover Image etc. The more the content on the Page or Group the better it is in terms of making it appear genuine and helpful.

- Create some appealing Content which you can put in as pinned post in the Group and Pages. This should basically tell the people about the benefits of joining the community and also appeal them to invite their friends to the forum.

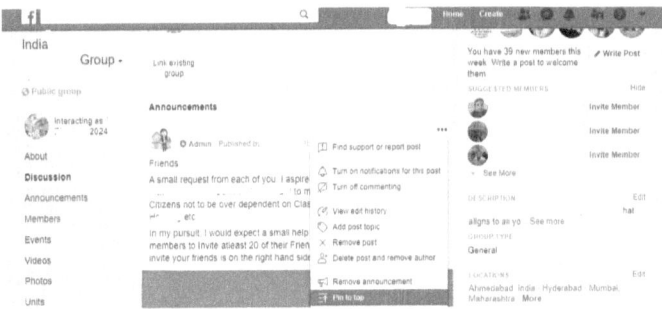

- Now comes the important step of linking all your Pages to the Group that you want to grow. This can be done by visiting the Page that you want to link. Once on the Page you will find the Groups section on the left hand Tab (if the Groups section does not appear by default, then get it added by visiting the settings of the Page). On clicking on the Groups section you will find the option to link your Page to your Group.

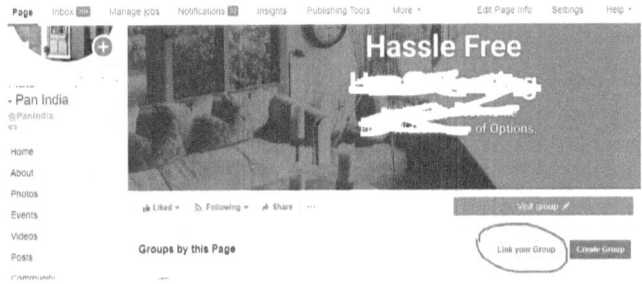

- You can also set and link your CTA button which appears on the Page to visit your Group. The button selected needs to be 'Visit Group'.

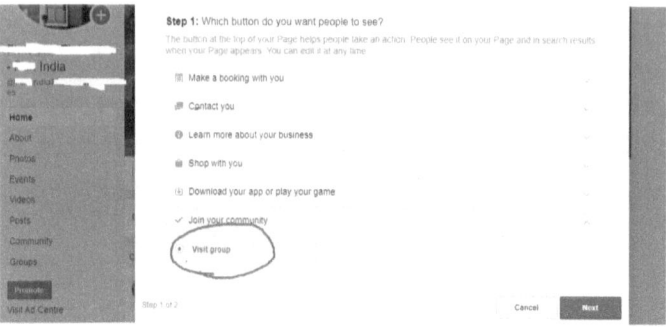

- Similarly follow the above steps to link all your Pages to the Group.

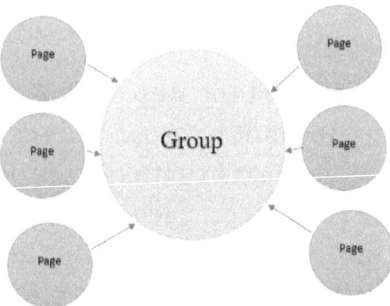

- All the Pages which were linked will now be appearing in the linked pages section on visiting the Group settings.

- Now having done all the hard work comes the final step of inviting all the members of your linked Pages (people who have liked your pages) to be a part of your Group. For that you have to first select the Page whose members you want to invite. This can be done by clicking on 'Interacting as' option on the left hand side top of the Group screen.

- Once you have selected the Page from which you are inter-acting in the Group, now comes the final step of inviting individual members who had liked the Page to be members of the Group. This section can be found on the right hand side of the Group screen. Note you won't be allowed to Invite all the members in one go, but you have to be consistent about inviting 30-40 members from each page on a daily basis to be part of the Group. This will ensure your Group grows organically at a healthy rate without spending any marketing dollars.

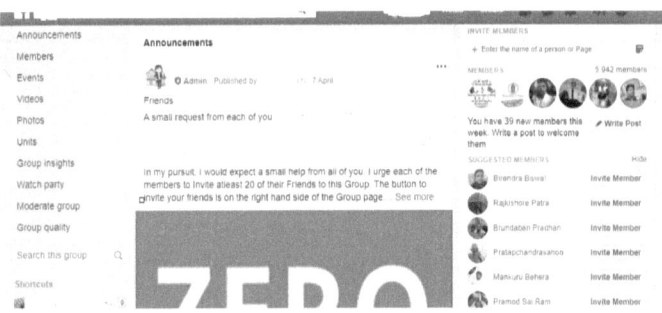

CHAPTER 8: BEST PRACTICES FOR FACEBOOK ADS

Having explored a way for organic traffic building through Facebook in the previous chapter, I would throw some light into some of the best practices from my personal experience when it comes to Paid Ads through Facebook. I would like to touch upon two aspects of Facebook Paid Ads.

- *Audience*

  Though Facebook gives you the option to target audience set by demographics, interests or behavior, the most effective means of targeting which I have found over the years is targeting by the custom audience feature. This makes the pointers I had highlighted on 'Chapter 2: Building Relevant Audience' all the more important as without executing it, one will not be able to utilize the Custom Audience feature.

  Email id and phone numbers are the most common attributes on the basis of which Facebook builds the custom audience lists. The beauty about this feature is you make sure you showcase your Ads to only the relevant audience set instead of wasting your marketing dollars on any random audience. It's a direct laser sharp approach given the fact that you have done your homework well when it comes to 'Building Relevant Audience'.

Once you have your custom audience ready and you select them as your targeted audience set for your Ad, do not forget to add your already existing customers whom you do not want to target in the exclude list. The reason is fairly simple, not to waste marketing dollars on acquiring customers who are already using your products. This segment needs to be engaged through other means rather than customer acquisition marketing ads.

- *Types of Ad*

The most appealing Ad format which I have found on Facebook over the years are the Carousel Ads. Going by my personal experience, Carousel Ads targeted at custom audience with an exclude audience list is a lethal combo in terms of optimized Ads with a very high conversion rate. It's important to add and mention about the product's USP (Unique Selling Point) or value proposition in coherence in the various frames of Carousel Ads.

- *Competitor Ads*

Checking out your competitors Ad periodically on Facebook can actually help you tap onto some leads at no cost.

Once you check out a few of your competitors Ads & like some of the Pages related to your industry, Facebook will automatically target you for all other similar kinds of interest based targeted Ads.

Once you click on the comments section in those Ads you can find your potential customers whom you can reach out to on Whatsapp once you have their email Id or phone no. In case you are not able to get their contact info you can connect with them on Facebook Messenger itself.

CHAPTER 9: SMS - AN UNDERRATED BUT POWERFUL TOOL

SMS happens to be my most favorite Tool when it comes to user acquisitions. Strange isn't it ? Well the reason is simple, it's a really cost effective medium and if utilized in the right way it can give you a high ROI. Early stage startups do not have the luxury to spend millions of dollars in marketing on Facebook & Google platforms. This makes SMS a highly convenient medium for them to scale initially till they attain the stage of being VC funded. I do believe it is a highly underrated and ignored medium. In this segment I will touch upon a few aspects by which you can make the most out of SMS.

- *Content*

    Content of your text message remains the key. Here are some tips for generating appealing content on text message,

    - Your message should be crisp and to the point

    - Include a Hook and CTA

    - Energy should be oozing out of your words (hypothetically), and the reader should feel it. It cannot be a dull mundane message, nobody really cares to reach the CTA stage for them.

    - Add line breakers (separate lines) to add more clarity to the message

    - Experiment and play around with content to identify the communication which is striking a chord with your audience. Once you are able to identify it, make sure you double down on it.

    - Quote numbers and figures wherever you can, this will

make your message powerful

- *Sender Id*

Sender Id is something you can play around with for acquiring customers effectively. Many times organizations prefer to use a standard Sender Id to communicate their messages. Well, when it comes to conveying any particular message or info to your existing customer base then this practise of a standard Sender Id is sound, but when it comes to new user acquisitions I would recommend you to create, try out and experiment with Sender Ids.

Make sure the Sender Id you are creating is really appealing to your customer base. Some examples of appealing 6 letters (as mandated by authorities in India) Sender Id can be 'Client', 'Leadss', 'Custmr', 'Dealzz' etc. This can vary from industry to industry depending on the target segment. Also trying out different Sender Ids will ensure that you are not spamming your audience base with messages piling on a single thread.

- *Audience*

Do not go overboard with SMS's as this can be spammy. Make sure you are regularly switching between audiences to ensure a particular individual is not getting your messages too often.

CHAPTER 10: KEY FEATURES OF WHATSAPP

U ndoubtedly Whatsapp is the most popular communication tool used today, but when it comes to using Whatsapp for professional purposes, it has its own set of limitations. In this segment I will discuss some of the really cool Whatsapp features which I have personally found immensely useful for professional communications to customers.

- *Bulk Importing Contacts to Gmail*

This one is not exactly a Whatsapp feature, but when integrated with Whatsapp it can be very powerful.

You can save names, email addresses, phone numbers and more fields in Google Contacts.

Contacts saved to your Google Account will sync with Google Contacts and all your Android devices. The steps that needs to be followed for this are,

Step 1: Compile the contacts you want to import on an Excel spreadsheet. Make sure your column headings are in row 1 and your first contact is in row 2. Column heading can be Name, Phone etc.

Step 2: Once you have put in all the column headings and contacts, save the file as CSV (Comma Separated Value).

Step 3: Open your Google contacts in Gmail and click on Create Contact. Choose the option Create Multiple Contacts.

Step 4: Once you click on Create Multiple Contacts, you will find the option to import contacts via CSV. So go ahead and import your file.

Step 5: Once you have imported the file, sync contacts on your phone by going to your phone settings and then sync Whatsapp to find all the Contacts you want to reach out to on your Whatsapp list.

Now that you have all your potential customers in your Whatsapp contacts, you can compose a smart message and reach out to them one to one. Before importing, you can also name the people on the CSV file in a way which can be easier for you to find them on your Whatsapp list and reach out to them. For example, you can name them as Customer 1, Customer 2 etc and search them by keyword 'Customer' on Whatsapp to find them. Make sure you do not go too overboard with it, do it in a slow and steady manner rather than reaching all the contacts in one go.

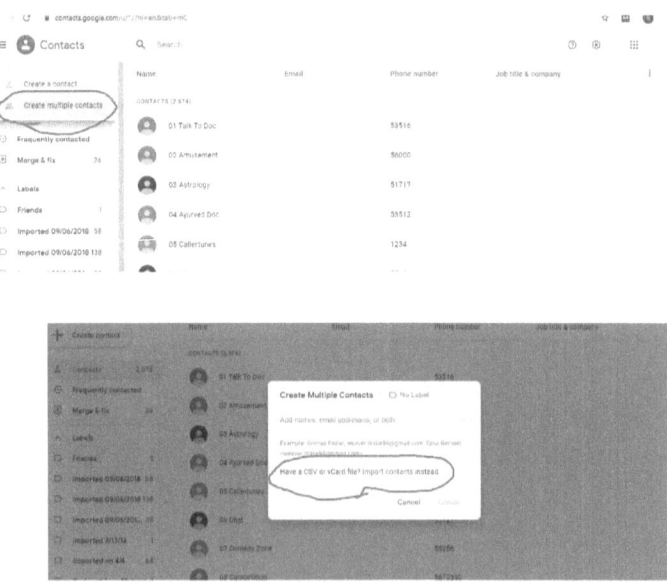

- *Restricted Whatsapp Groups*

The restricted Whatsapp Groups where the admins are only

allowed to post, are particularly important when you want to convey important communication messages to your audience or customer base. It is difficult to regulate the messages in general Whatsapp Groups and often it becomes too spammy. That is the reason Whatsapp came out with this feature where you can change any Group to a restricted Group from the Group settings. Some pointers to take note while creating such Groups are,

- Put up a nice professional image as Group icon. It can also be your organization's logo.

- Put up a nicely written Group description with a link to check out more details about your product or organization or anything you want to showcase to your customers.

- Just after creating the Group, put in a welcome message in the Group also mentioning the purpose for which the Group has been created.

- Often it is a good practise to also post a FAQ list in the Group to answer most of the participants queries.

- Do convey to the participants that they can reach out to you separately on personal windows for any queries and be prepared to answer them yourselves or get them answered by a chat operator.

- Use Bold (*XYZ*) and Italics (_XYZ_) wherever necessary in the texts to deliver an impactful communication.

- *Click to Chat Feature*

WhatsApp's click to chat feature allows you to begin a chat with someone without having their phone number saved in your phone's address book. As long as you know this person's phone number and they have an active WhatsApp account, you can create a link that will allow you to start a chat with them. By clicking the link, a chat with the person automatically opens.

You can propage the Link using SMS or any other medium among your target audience and ask them to click on the link to reach out to you on Whatsapp. By doing so you are ensuring a two way communication happening between you and your potential customer. The challenge lies in eliciting an initial response from your target segment which this feature has been able to solve to a great extent as people are generally comfortable in communicating via the Whatsapp medium. You can refer to the link to know details about How to use click to chat .

CHAPTER 11: UNLEASHING THE POWER OF LINKEDIN

L inkedIn in general has a perception of being a B2B specific and a costly marketing channel. This is true to some extent but that does not mean B2C business can't benefit from LinkedIn. LinkedIn does help you and your business immensely in various aspects. I would be discussing in detail about two of such aspects in this segment.

- *Personal & Organizational Brand Building*

    It's imperative for Startup founders to build their personal brand along with their organizational brand if they want to catch the eye of the top Venture Capitalists in the shorter or longer run. So here are some pointers I would like to share which you should keep into account while building your personal brand as it is directly linked to building your organizational brand,

    - **Profile Optimization:** It is important to optimize your profile for LinkedIn SEO the way we do it on Google for your website. Some components of a optimized profile are,

        ➢ Catchy LinkedIn Profile Headline

        ➢ Descriptive Profile Summary

        ➢ Professional Profile Image

        ➢ Work Experience section highlighting all your previous engagements with media links wherever applicable

        ➢ Recommendations from your previous employers or mentors

> ➤ You can use the Featured section in your Profile to put up media articles or your website links. This can be used as CTA to drive traffic or for brand building.

All the above components need to be optimized taking into account the keyword for which you want to rank for, it can be something like 'Internet Entrepreneur' , 'Tech Startup' etc.

- **Creating Great Content:** This is something which is really critical if you want to build your personal or professional brand. There are thousands of content pieces getting created everyday and being shared, in order to stand out from the crowd your content needs to have the magic touch. Some components of creating valuable and eye catchy content are,

  > ➤ Only create something (content) if you truly believe it is going to add value to the readers.

  > ➤ Make sure you catch the attention of the reader in the initial 2 lines, as to view the texts from 3rd line onwards you have to click on 'See More' on LinkedIn. Clicking on 'see more' is regarded as an engagement signal by LinkedIn which should make your Post gain more views.

  > ➤ Pen down in depth and longer posts, but break it down in various paras or shorter sections to make it easily readable.

  > ➤ Do mention about your business wherever you can in the post, but do not add your web link on the post itself as LinkedIn does not prefer the readers to go out of their platform to an external site. You can post the link to your website as a comment to the Post.

➢ Comments are more effective than likes to expand your post views.

➢ Do regularly share content from your Company Page as well. You can use the invite option in the Company Page to invite people who are more likely to like your Page and actively engage with your content.

- *Connection Building for Sales and Funding*

LinkedIn can be a really effective medium if you want to leverage it for B2B Sales or for reaching out to Venture Capitalists or potential Investors. The key here lies in identifying the right set of people and connecting with them.

• **Searching for the right Connections:** To find the right connections in limited iterations one can make use of Boolean searches. By Boolean searches I mean, combining two separate searches by a connecting word like 'and', 'in' etc. For example, one can combine two searches together to make a single search like 'Head of growth in Gurgaon'. Here you are combining search via designation and location to make it a single search. You can also check out the Linkedin Boolean Search Tool to assist you with carrying out Boolean Searches.

Many of you might be facing the problem of limited searches due to non premium LinkedIn accounts. To overcome this issue, you can carry out your searches in Google in the similar manner as you were doing it on LinkedIn as all the LinkedIn Profiles are crawled and appear as separate web links on Google Search. You can also take the assistance of Linkedin Unlimited Searches Tool to help you in this regard.

- **Establishing Connection:** Now that you have identi-fied your target segment whom you want to reach out to, the next step is establishing successful connections with them. Few pointers you can take note to ensure your connections are successfully accepted,

  ➢ Always send a personalized connection message

  ➢ Your connection message needs to be succinct and to the point

  ➢ Ensure the gist of the communication is present in the initial 1-2 lines

  ➢ Your message should sound interesting and not mundane. The other person needs to be equally excited in getting to know you or your organiza-tion.

  ➢ Always follow up wherever necessary

CHAPTER 12: BEST PRACTICES ON GOOGLE

C overing Google and its products in totality needs an entire book to be penned down on the subject, but nonetheless I will reflect upon a few best practices that I have come across while dealing with Google and its wide array of products.

- *Google Search*

    This is the most important tool in the digital world according to me. If you are aware of the power of Google Search, then I would say you have partially conquered the topic Digital Marketing. Everything and anything is available on the net nowadays, you just need to make the right search to come across it. Find a few pointers which can be help you while doing a Google Search,

    - If you are searching for something in document or PDF format, mention the word PDF along with your primary search word.

    - Adding 'inurl:' at the beginning to your search keyword can help you to find pages with the search keyword in the URL. Example, 'inurl:apple' will return any results containing the word "apple" in the URL.

    - Adding 'intext:' at the beginning to your search keyword can help you to find pages with the search keyword in the Page Content. Example, 'intext:apple' will return any results containing the word "apple" in the Page Content.

    - Always experiment and try out different variations of what your primary keyword to come across the desired results you are searching for.

- *Google Play Store*

If you are an App based business, then it is highly imperative for you to optimize your App for making it searchable on Playstore. This is the App version of SEO and termed as ASO - App Search Optimization and is really important if you want to keep your cost per acquisition in check by increasing your Organic Installs. A few factors that you need to take care for helping you in ASO are,

- Your target keyword should appear in the App name.

- Make the App description as in depth and descriptive as possible.

- App description should contain your target keyword and semantics of it.

- App Images should be uploaded in a coherent manner and should be appealing.

- Ratings and Reviews are a key component of ASO. Google gives it a high weightage along with the last 24 hours App install numbers when it comes to ranking factors. There are several ways in which you can manage your ratings and reviews which I would like to throw some light upon,

  ➤ Use the power of the network to pump up your ratings. They can be employees, friends or families. Here is a little trick to nail it. You do not need to download an App to be able to rate it. You can click on Install and then cancel the App installation midway. Now you will be able to successfully rate the App without even installing it. You can share this info among your network whom you want to leverage.

➢ Make sure when you are asking anyone to rate the App do suggest them a few keywords as well wherever possible. These keywords should be from the list of keywords you want to rank for.

➢ You can also ask your happy customers to rate you on Playstore via the product. Create an in App pop up which asks your users whether 'they are loving the App' ? This should have two options or buttons - the positive responses get directed to Play Store requesting them to rate the App and the negative ones can be directed and asked to submit their feedback over mail.

➢ Make sure you respond to all the ratings and reviews. Try to convert the bad ones to good reviews by effective customer support and grievance handling.

- *Google Ads*

I would like to touch upon two particular features in Adwords which I have found particularly effective.

- **Custom Audience**: Like Facebook, Google too provides you the option of targeting customers via custom audience feature by uploading the info of your target segment. This ensures targeted marketing and keeps the marketing costs under check. At this point I would again reiterate the importance of Chapter 3: Building Relevant Audience.

- **Remarketing:** Remarketing is a really powerful feature for converting the customers who are in a 50:50 state of mind. You can make use of remarketing Ads to reinforce your product communication to convert these set of customers.

You can go through the following articles to successfully create and target remarketing audiences.

Create a website remarketing list - Google Ads Help

Create yourfirst display remarketing campaign - Google Ads Help

When it comes to App, Play Store won't allow you to place a cookie in order to tap the set of customers who had clicked on the Install button but had not downloaded the App or had dropped off midway. In order to tap this segment you can do a little hack,

Step 1: Place the remarketing cookie on a 3rd party page

Step 2: Create a link which first takes you to the 3rd party page and anyone who lands on that page gets redirected to your App page on Play Store.

Step 3: Propagate the link along with your marketing message using SMS and Facebook marketing channels.

Step 4: This way you can ensure that you build on your remarketing audience due to the cookie placement on the 3rd party page and subsequent redirection to Play Store.

- *Useful Tools from Google*

• Google Trends: For analyzing the popularity of top search queries in Google Search across various regions and languages using graphs to compare the search volume of different queries over time.

• Google Market Finder: For identifying new international business opportunities using market insights.

• Google Webmasters: For tracking your site's search

performance and optimizing for SEO.

- Google Analytics: For tracking and reporting website traffic

- Google My Business: For promoting your business for free and tapping into key google search keywords by optimizing your Google business page name accordingly. This can also help you in tapping the 'Near me' type of keywords which are really popular these days.

CHAPTER 13: CATCHING THE EYE OF VC'S

L et's say you have done all the hard work in the right way to power your Startup from the 1 to 1 Million users stage, so What Next ?

Now you need fresh capital to scale your startup further and take it to 1 Billion valuation, unless and until you are determined and intend to remain bootstrapped. Remaining bootstrapped is the best possible thing as you do not really need to dilute your equity. But for all practical purposes for giving shape to your vision and building an unicorn, most of the startup founders do seek out VC funded capital. Now that you have decided that you need capital, What Next ?

Now you have to compete with thousands of founders like you who are actively chasing out VC's. You need to stand out of the crowd with a superior product. Your product should be the game changer to help you outcompete all your competitors around. Apart from a superior product, you need to have a compelling story of your Startup journey. Few pointers that you need to take into account while building up a compelling story,

- What was the idea for the startup ?

- Which specific problem are you trying to solve ?

- What have you done to solve the problem ? Basically Your startup journey.

- User problems you have solved till now ?

- What is the next problem you intend to solve by your product ?

- How do you intend to solve the problem ? What will be your approach ?

- What are your expansion plans ?

Your story needs to be ably supported by your key growth metrics. Numbers are really crucial to back your story. Do use the power of the media to propagate your story to the world. Do some PR, share some media articles along with customer testimonial videos on social media, jot down some blog articles and you need to do all these consistently for some time. You can also try to arrange for database of journalists and media persons and target them specifically on Facebook and Google showcasing your articles.

Now that you have all the checklists in place, you can expect some in bound queries and interests from the VC circuit. Ideally you should not be chasing them, but it should be the other way out. Once it starts happening, congratulations my friend you are well on your way to multiply your startup valuations.

CONCLUSION

Now that you have gone through the entire booklet, I would advise you only one thing before I wind up.

There is no secret sauce which can really spice up your startup from 1 to $10^{6}X$ stage overnight. It's all about following the best practices, learning new stuffs from every possible source and most importantly executing them. Keep executing and keep experimenting till you hit the right note. Once you execute and do it yourselves, you will have the confidence and once you gain the confidence then there is nothing stopping you. You will march ahead along with your startup.

I hope with this handbook which happens to be my first, I have been able to add some value in your and your startup's journey. Will be looking forward for all your feedbacks and reviews which will surely help me improve in the near future. From my end I will make sure I do respond to each of your reviews. Thank you once again for having bought this handbook and giving it a read.

Cheers

Amar

ABOUT THE AUTHOR

Amar Jyoti

Amar is a startup enthusiast and a growth hacker with a keen appetite to learn and grow with every single day. He started his career with some of India's top Brands - Tata Technologies & ICICI Bank. But his inclination towards startup hustle dragged him out of the steady corporate world.

He was a core founding member and at quite an early age had donned the hat of 'Head of Growth' in a home rental tech startup - Fastfox.com, which eventually got acquired at 1 Billion Valuation. Post Fastfox he has been heading the growth vertical in some of the India's top mid sized startups like Housing.com, Square Yards and leading them in their growth Path.

He has a keen interest in politics and had also undertaken a political consultancy stint working in close tandem with an union minister of India. Amar is an electrical engineering graduate from NIT Surat and also holds a masters degree.

You can reach out to him anytime on LinkedIn or drop a mail on amar.nitsurat@gmail.com for any queries, suggestions, feedback or anything.